S0-CVJ-936

# The Greyhound

## by William R. Sanford and Carl R. Green

CRESTWOOD HOUSE

New York

# CIP

## LIBRARY OF CONGRESS CATALOGING IN PUBLICATION DATA

Sanford, William R. (William Reynolds)
  Greyhound

  (Top dog)
  Includes index.
  SUMMARY: Discusses the history, physical characteristics, care, and breeding of this hound known for its tremendous speed.
    1. Greyhounds — Juvenile literature. [1. Greyhounds. 2. Dogs.] I. Green, Carl R. II. Title. III. Series: Sanford, William R. (William Reynolds), Top dog.
  SF429.G8S36       1989            636.7'53 — dc20                    89-31113
  ISBN 0-89686-450-2

# PHOTO CREDITS

Cover: Reynolds Photography: Larry Reynolds
Animals Animals: (M. Conte) 11; (R. Kolar) 40
Photri: 21, 37, 41; (L. Riess) 45
Third Coast Stock Source: (D & I MacDonald) 7, 32, 42
Reynolds Photography: (Larry Reynolds) 4, 13, 14, 19, 27

Copyright © 1989 by Crestwood House, Macmillan Publishing Company

Macmillan Publishing Company
866 Third Avenue
New York, NY 10022
Collier Macmillan Canada, Inc.

Produced by Carnival Enterprises

Printed in the United States of America

First Edition

10  9  8  7  6  5  4  3  2  1

# TABLE OF
# CONTENTS

# FOR MORE
# INFORMATION

For more information about greyhounds, write to:

American Kennel Club
51 Madison Avenue
New York, NY 10010

Greyhound Club of America
334 King Street
P.O. Box 1185
Hanover, MA 02339

# GREYHOUND RACING IS BIG BUSINESS

The Oklahoma sun was bright and warm when Teresa entered the kennels. In each wire run, she saw tall, lean dogs. "Even when they're standing still, greyhounds look fast," she said to herself.

"Hi," a woman's voice called. "You must be Teresa. I'm Janet Clark. Welcome to Fleet-wing Kennels."

Teresa turned and shook hands. "Hello, Mrs. Clark," she said. "Thanks for taking the time to talk to me. As I told you on the phone, I'm writing a report about greyhounds."

"I'm happy to talk to anyone who's interested in my dogs," the woman said.

Teresa looked at her notes. "How many dogs do you have here?" she asked.

"We raise about 150 greyhounds a year," Mrs. Clark replied. "As you can see, this is a big operation. It costs about $1,500 to prepare a greyhound for its first race."

"That's a lot of money!" Teresa exclaimed.

*The sleek, streamlined greyhound has been bred for at least 5,000 years.*

"If I wanted to buy a good racer, would I have to pay that much?"

Mrs. Clark put her head back and laughed. "You can't touch a quality dog for less than $3,000," she said. "If the dog shapes up well in training, the bidding can go as high as $15,000. You have to remember, though, that many of our dogs never make it as racers. We sell the nonstarters as pets for about $300."

"Three thousand dollars is a lot of money for a dog," Teresa said, shaking her head. She wrote the numbers in her notebook.

"Some people own as many as 40 greyhounds," Mrs. Clark said. "Their dogs race at many different tracks, and they make a good living that way. The easiest way to get into racing is to find some partners who will share the cost of one or two good dogs. The partners get 35 percent of the prize money, and their trainer keeps the rest. That pays for the dogs' room and board."

"Do the dogs race for big prizes?" Teresa asked.

"No, it's just the opposite," Mrs. Clark said. "At a small track, a dog may win as little as $50 for finishing first. The big tracks pay purses from $500 to $1,000. The richest race of all, the Greyhound Race of Champions, is another story. The winner of the 1988 race

*Race-quality greyhounds can be sold by breeders for as much as $15,000.*

won $60,000! To make up for the small purses, each greyhound races several times a week. The top dogs do very well. A famous greyhound named Marathon Hound won $225,000 before his owner retired him in 1984."

Teresa's pencil was flying across the paper. "What happens when a greyhound can't race anymore?" she asked.

"My son can answer that question," Mrs. Clark said. She called to a boy who was cleaning a nearby kennel run.

Willie put down his mop and joined them. "In the old days, trainers destroyed their dogs when they stopped winning," he explained. "That was tragic, because most of them would have made fine pets. Now, the NGA—the National Greyhound Association—helps find new owners for them."

Teresa wrote some more and then asked, "Can I meet some of your greyhounds now? I want to learn everything I can about these beautiful dogs."

# AN OLD AND HONORED BREED

The greyhound has been *bred* for its speed and courage for at least 5,000 years. In Egyptian tomb paintings from 3000 B.C., lean, long-legged greyhounds stand beside the pharaohs. In other paintings, the Egyptian god Anubis appears with a greyhoundlike head. Anubis was the god who guided the soul on its journey to the land of the dead. Similar pictures of greyhounds appear in the artwork of other early cultures.

No one knows exactly how the greyhound earned its name. Some experts believe the name is from the word *great*. In this sense, it means that greyhounds were owned by nobles and other "great" people. It's also possible the name comes from the word *gazehound*. Gazehound means a dog that tracks game by sight rather than by scent. Perhaps the best answer is also the simplest. The breed may have been named for its most common coat color—*grey*.

In A.D. 1016, Britain's King Canute signed a law that made it illegal for common people to own greyhounds. Canute wanted to protect the royal game preserves. He knew the hunting ability of these dogs. No one was allowed to keep a greyhound within ten miles of a royal forest. Killing a greyhound was even more serious. The penalty was death!

By the 1400s, greyhounds were part of everyday life in Britain. William Shakespeare mentioned greyhounds in his history play, *Henry V.* He wrote: "I see you standing like greyhounds in the slips, straining upon the start—the game's on foot." Shakespeare was probably referring to the sport of *coursing*. In a coursing match, two dogs are sent after a hare. The winner is the dog that catches the hare or comes closest to catching it.

For many years, greyhounds were bred with

smooth coats and rough coats. In the mid-1700s, thanks to a Lord Orford, the smooth-coated dogs won out. Orford crossed his greyhounds with the long-legged English bulldogs. His breeding produced a long-nosed dog. The dog had the greyhound's speed and the bulldog's courage. Orford's greyhounds had grey coats flecked with black, a color known as *brindle.*

The Spanish brought the first greyhounds to North America in the 1500s. Two hundred years later, a greyhound took part in the American Revolution. General Friedrich von Steuben kept a greyhound at his side while he trained American troops at Valley Forge. In the 1800s, General George Custer often traveled with a pack of 40 greyhounds and staghounds. Custer's dogs weren't with him, though, when his cavalry unit was wiped out at the battle of the Little Big Horn in 1876.

The greyhound's popularity grows out of the many roles it plays. As a coursing dog, the greyhound's speed makes it a favorite with hunters of small game. As a *show dog,* the greyhound has been winning blue ribbons ever since the first Westminster Kennel Club show in 1877. The sport of greyhound racing took off after O. P. Smith invented the mechanical rabbit in 1912. Greyhounds chase this fake

*Today's greyhounds have many cousins, including the rare Italian greyhound.*

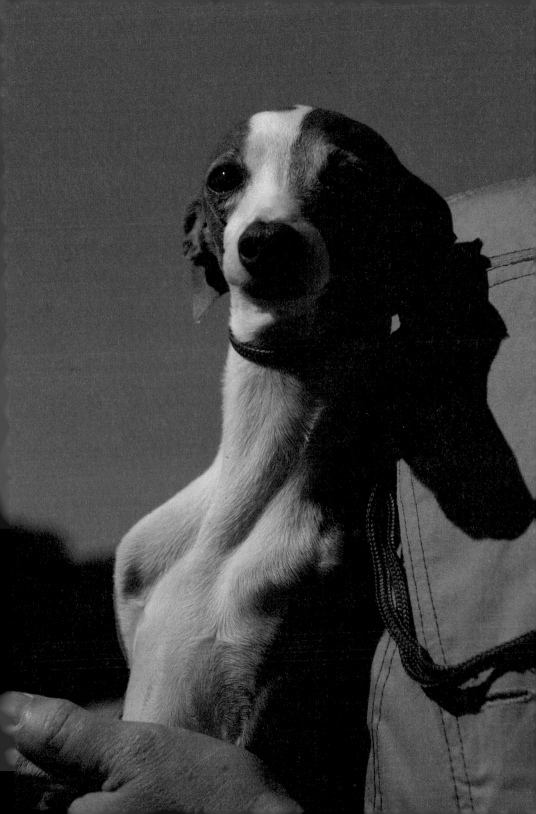

rabbit around a racetrack. Finally, as family pets, greyhounds are clean, loyal, and affectionate. People who own them believe no other dog can match them in looks or in temperament.

# THE GREYHOUND IN CLOSE-UP

The greyhound belongs to a family of hounds that has been bred for speed. In addition to the greyhound, these hunting dogs include the whippet (the smallest), the saluki (the fastest), and the Irish wolfhound (the tallest of all dogs). The greyhound is better known than any of the others. Mention speed or racing, and people think first of greyhounds.

The greyhound's slender appearance can be deceiving. An adult male stands between 28 and 30 inches at the *withers* (the top of the shoulder). That's as tall as a Saint Bernard. The same male weighs from 65 to 70 pounds. Females are about an inch shorter and may

*Although most greyhounds have a solid-color coat, white or black markings are also common.*

weigh as much as 20 pounds less. Racing dogs are usually heavier than show dogs. A great Irish racer named Rebel Light weighed in at 90 pounds.

The greyhound's short, nearly waterproof coat comes in many colors. If you go to a dog track, you'll see grey, black, blue, red, tan, brindle, and white greyhounds. Most dogs have a solid-color coat. White or black markings are also common. For greyhounds competing at a dog show, any color is acceptable.

*The long, thin head of a greyhound narrows to a nearly pointed muzzle.*

Every part of the greyhound seems to be streamlined. The head is long and narrow. It tapers from a broad skull to a nearly pointed *muzzle*. The jaw is level and the teeth meet in a true scissors bite. The dark eyes are widely spaced and bulge only slightly. When it's running, the dog folds its small, rose-shaped ears flat against its head. The strong, arched neck is anchored in well-muscled shoulders and a broad chest. All four legs are slender and straight. The long, thin tail serves as a rudder when the dog is running at full speed. At rest,

14

the tail is carried down, with a slight upward curve.

The greyhound's internal anatomy is similar to that of other dogs. At four months, its baby teeth are replaced by 42 adult teeth. The first teeth people notice are the long, sharp *canines*. The dog uses its canines for holding and tearing. The other teeth are *incisors* (cutting teeth), *molars,* and *premolars* (slicing and crushing teeth). Despite this mouthful of teeth, the greyhound doesn't chew its food. When a piece of meat is small enough to swallow, the dog gulps it down.

Even at rest, a greyhound looks ready for action. Let a rabbit loose where the dog can see it, and watch out! As it begins its gallop, the greyhound pushes forward off its powerful hind legs. The front legs stretch out and touch the ground at the end of the leap. One leg is in front of the other. The front legs absorb the shock and propel the dog forward. Meanwhile, the hind legs are preparing for the next great bound.

As you might guess, greyhounds hold records for speed and jumping. A greyhound can reach 38 miles per hour in a 660-yard race. The record for the long jump is held by a greyhound named Bang, who jumped 30 feet while chasing a hare.

# A SIGHT HOUND WITH A KEEN NOSE

Are dogs smart? Scientists say no and point to the small size of the dog's brain. At about four ounces, a greyhound's brain cannot produce high-level thought. You can teach a dog to sit up and beg, for example, but only after many repetitions.

On the other hand, dogs sometimes show surprising talents. The owner of one greyhound, for example, claimed it could add simple numbers. When the owner said, "Add three and two," the dog moved its front paw five times and stopped. Given more problems, the dog answered correctly every time. The "trick" was discovered when the owner was asked to step behind a screen before giving the commands. When it heard the new problems, the greyhound became confused. It waved its paw aimlessly, stopping at almost any number but the correct answer. The experiment showed the dog wasn't a math genius. It was expert at "reading" human faces. Without knowing it, the owner's eyes were giving a "stop" signal to the dog when it reached the right number.

Although greyhounds hunt by sight, their eyes probably aren't any better than those of other dogs. If a distant rabbit or deer stays still, the dog won't recognize it by shape alone. Only when the animal moves will the greyhound give chase. A dog's eyesight is different than yours in other ways, too. Dogs are colorblind, and their close-up vision is poor. They do see a wider field of view, and they have excellent night vision.

If a dog's eyesight is only average, its hearing is superior to that of humans. Dogs hear a wider range of sounds, and they also hear fainter sounds. The greyhound's erect ears move freely to zero in on the source of any noise. The human ear hears sounds up to 20,000 cycles a second. But greyhounds can hear up to 70,000 cycles a second. Dogs hear best in the range of 40,000 cycles, which is twice the level of most human speech. Perhaps that's why a dog responds more quickly to a sharp whistle than to the sound of someone calling its name.

Even though they hunt by sight, greyhounds depend heavily on their sense of smell. Watch a greyhound as it sniffs at a fire hydrant. Its nose is "reading" the odors. The flood of molecules that excite its *olfactory patch* sends very specific messages to the brain. If the dog could speak, it could tell you whether the dogs that passed the hydrant today were male or female, sick or well, fully fed or hungry. With proper training, the greyhound could track any of the dogs to its home.

The dog's senses of taste and touch are less developed. A greyhound can taste salty, sweet, and sour flavors. It's the scent, however, that tells a dog whether or not the food is worth eating. The dog's whiskers are highly responsive to touch, but its skin is much less sensitive. That doesn't mean that a dog doesn't feel your hand on its back. Stroke a greyhound's smooth coat, and you'll feel the animal quiver with pleasure. These are "people" dogs. They delight in your company.

# MORE THAN A RACING DOG

Almost everyone thinks of greyhounds as racing dogs. As a result, few people think of them as pets. That's too bad because the greyhound is an excellent family dog. It is gentle

*Greyhounds are clean, loyal, and affectionate pets.*

and loving with the people who feed and care for it. The dog responds well to discipline and is easy to train.

More than many dogs, the greyhound prefers to stay at the side of its owner. These dogs take a long time to warm up to strangers. Arrian, a Roman who lived around A.D. 200, was an admirer of the breed. He wrote that his greyhound was his constant friend at home. His dog was also an alert escort on long trips. When Arrian was gone for a short time, the dog jumped up to greet him on his return. The modern greyhound behaves in exactly the same way.

As long as they have room to exercise, greyhounds are easy to keep. Because they're clean dogs, they seldom develop a "doggy" odor. Since they have short coats, *shedding* is not a major problem. Greyhounds walk through crowded rooms without knocking into furniture. They need only a small space for sleeping. On a farm or ranch, a greyhound comes into its own. It can catch more rats than a cat. It can clear out the local rabbits before they can damage the garden.

A 70-pound greyhound isn't for everyone. The dog's size makes it a poor choice for people who live in small apartments. Out on the street, the breed's instincts lead it to chase anything that moves. That behavior can turn a quiet walk into a breakneck run after the neighbor's cat. It takes a strong arm and a stout *choke chain* to keep a greyhound from running away from you. In addition, the greyhound likes to be treated as an individual. Each one is different.

Some people say the greyhound becomes mean when it meets other dogs. In most cases, it's more likely to ignore the strange dog than to attack it. Racing greyhounds do wear muzzles, but that's to keep them from nipping each other during the races.

*While they race, greyhounds wear muzzles so they don't bite other dogs racing near them.*

People who know the breed say there's something almost human about greyhounds. Like people, these dogs are easy to spoil. A traveler once visited a small racing kennel in Ireland. The owners fed eggs and cream to their dogs, even though they couldn't afford these luxuries for themselves. When the visitor entered the house, he found two greyhounds resting on the beds. The owners were sitting on the floor!

Spoiled or not, a greyhound will reward your care with undying love. It will run for you, hunt for you, and cheer you up when you're sad. What more could you ask of a dog?

# CHOOSING A GREYHOUND PUPPY

Before you choose a greyhound *puppy*, you should know why you want the dog. People own this special breed for many different reasons. Which one applies to you?

You want a well-mannered family pet, but you don't want just any dog. You're attracted to the greyhound because of its clean, good looks and competitive spirit.

You want to win blue ribbons by showing your greyhound. You plan to train the dog for the show ring, not the racetrack.

You plan to compete in coursing events or in dog racing. You know racing is tough, but you're sure you and your dog can overcome the odds.

You want to raise greyhounds for fun and profit. You're willing to pay a good price for the best female available.

Once you know why you want to own a greyhound, you can begin the search for the perfect puppy. Here are some useful rules:

*Buy your dog from a quality breeder.* The cheapest dog probably isn't the best dog. Talk to people who know greyhounds. Find out who the best breeders are. Visit the kennels near you and study the mother of a *litter* as carefully as you study the puppies. If the breeder also owns the male who fathered the litter, check him over, too. You can tell a lot about how a puppy will develop by looking at its parents. If you're buying a racing dog, attend the trials where young dogs are racing for the first time. If you can pick a winner when it's still young, you may save a lot of money.

*Pick a bold, healthy puppy.* Even experts

find it hard to select a future champion from a litter of puppies. It's not as difficult to pick a good pet-quality puppy. First, be sure the puppy has had its puppy shots. Its eyes should be clear and its nose should be cool and damp. Next, look for a puppy with a long neck, broad chest, and good feet. If a puppy passes these tests, try dragging a bag past its nose. At eight weeks, the puppy's chase *instinct* should send it running after the bag. Avoid any puppy that ignores the bag or acts scared.

*Be sure to ask for the puppy's papers.* A *purebred* greyhound should come with a full set of papers. This *pedigree* describes the dog's ancestry. If you don't have papers, you can't register the dog with one of the national kennel clubs. That means you won't be able to show or race the dog. In addition, you'll have trouble selling any puppies you raise.

*Buy your greyhound at the proper age.* A puppy should never leave its mother before it's eight weeks old. That's a good age to take a dog home for a family pet. If you're buying a racing dog, it's best to buy an older dog. No one can predict how well a puppy will run until it's nearly grown. A racer doesn't reach its peak until it's three or four years old. Finally, don't forget that older greyhounds make good pets, too. You can adopt a retired racing dog by contacting the National Greyhound Association in Abilene, Kansas.

# CARING FOR YOUR GREYHOUND

Anyone who spends $10,000 for a racing greyhound takes very good care of the dog. A poorly fed and carelessly trained dog will never win any races. Families that buy greyhounds as pets sometimes forget the same rules apply to them. A dog can't be a happy, healthy pet without proper diet, *grooming*, health care, and exercise.

Your greyhound puppy will need five meals a day at first, made up of milk, puppy meal, and ground meat. Breeders suggest you use goat's milk instead of cow's milk. The milk's higher fat content is closer to the 12 percent fat found in a greyhound's milk. As your puppy grows, increase the amount of food and decrease the number of feedings. Give it just as much as it'll eat and no more. When your greyhound is one year old, limit it to a single meal each day. A balanced diet of proteins, fats, and starches will keep any dog in good health.

Part of feeding a dog is learning what *not* to feed it. Most people know that small, splintery bones are dangerous. If you give your dog a chicken or fish bone, it's likely to catch in its throat and choke it. Feeding any dog sweets, such as candy or cookies, is bad as well. Dogs love sweet foods, but soon gain too much weight.

If you brush and comb your dog every day, it won't need many baths. Regular grooming stimulates a greyhound's skin and keeps the dog healthy. If a greyhound's coat has grown in too thickly, you can thin it out with a stripping comb. Some owners then use a special glove that has bristles attached. This "hound glove" allows you to brush and massage the dog in one ten-minute session. The brushing leaves the dog's coat shiny, while the massage keeps its muscles loose. Long, sweeping strokes are best. Don't rub too hard. Never dig into the muscles with your fingertips.

The average greyhound has a life span of 12 years. To make sure your greyhound lives that long, take it to a *veterinarian* for regular checkups. Along with keeping your dog's shots up to date, the vet will check it for *worms,* ear canker, and other problems. You'll know your dog has worms if it develops a potbelly or runny eyes, and if it vomits after eating. Worm medicine is powerful and is best handled by a vet. As for keeping your dog free of fleas, you might try an electronic flea collar. These devices put out high-pitched tones that seem to drive away fleas.

Greyhounds are large, active dogs. Racing dogs receive regular training, but family pets are sometimes overlooked. Set aside some time for exercise every day. Whenever possible, find an area where you can let your dog loose to run and play. Drag a bundle of rags

*Greyhounds need plenty of exercise. They especially like to run in wide-open spaces.*

behind your bicycle for it to chase. The run will keep your dog in good shape, and you'll have the joy of seeing a true running machine at work.

# TRAINING THE PET GREYHOUND

Have you ever walked into someone's house, only to be jumped on by the family's dog? As you try to push the dog away, the owner says, "Down, boy, down," in a soft voice. The dog keeps on jumping. He ignores the command. It's clear this dog hasn't been trained properly.

You want your greyhound to be well behaved. Indeed, that's the only way you and the dog can be happy together. Training should start the day you bring a new puppy home. All you need is patience and a few simple rules.

*Rule 1: Train with kindness and rewards.* Your dog wants to please you. *Reinforce* good behavior with a pat on the head or a dog biscuit. The dog will work overtime to earn more rewards.

*Rule 2: Be consistent.* Always reward good

behavior and scold bad behavior. Laughing at a naughty puppy one time and yelling at it the next will only confuse the dog.

*Rule 3: Begin each command with the dog's name.* Call your puppy by name and reward it when it responds. The puppy soon will come running every time you call. Better yet, hearing its name alerts the dog to the command that will follow.

*Rule 4: Repeat each lesson over and over.* Like all dogs, greyhounds seldom learn a new command the first time. Be ready to repeat the lesson until the dog gets it right. Once the dog learns what "Speedy, down!" means, it won't forget it.

*Rule 5: Keep the lessons short.* After five minutes, a puppy's attention starts to wander. Break off the lesson and play for a while. Then repeat the earlier lesson.

Now, let's apply these rules to a dog's basic training. *Housebreaking* begins with one of the dog's basic instincts: It doesn't want to soil the place where it sleeps. Start by fixing up a wire or wooden crate for the puppy. The crate will keep the puppy confined when you're not there to watch it. When the puppy wakes up from a nap, take it to a pile of newspapers near the back door. Praise it when it relieves itself on the papers. If the puppy has an accident, scold it and wash the spot with a strong cleaner to remove the odor. If you're patient and consistent, the puppy will soon seek out the papers. Later, use one of the damp newspapers to move the puppy to a new spot outdoors. The dog will quickly adjust to the new routine.

You can teach the puppy to come in a similar way. Attach a long cord to the young greyhound's collar. Take the dog outdoors and let it roam freely. As it's sniffing around, call "Speedy, come!" in a firm voice. Reward the dog if it returns to you. If it doesn't, give the cord a sharp jerk and force the dog to come to you. Keep the training session short, but repeat it daily until Speedy gets it right.

A book on dog training will give you more tips on how to teach other commands. Every dog should know "Heel" (walking at your left side), "Stay" (remain in one place), and "No bark" (be quiet, everything's okay). With these commands mastered, a greyhound is ready to go on to harder lessons.

# BREEDING AND RAISING PUPPIES

Letting a female dog have puppies by the first male that wanders by isn't breeding. What if your lovely Fireball mates with a neighbor's basset hound? A careful breeder chooses a *bitch* (as the female is called) with good ancestors. Then the breeder mates her to the best male (the *stud*) that's available.

Females first come into *heat* (the time they can become pregnant) at ten months. But they aren't ready to mate until 18 months. Let the vet check your dog before you mate her. Having puppies puts a heavy strain on the female's body.

If you want your puppies to be show dogs, select a champion show dog as the stud. To produce racing dogs, you'll have to find a champion racer. The easiest way to pay a high stud fee is to give the owner "the pick of the litter." You'll give up one puppy, but the rest will be yours to keep or sell. Fireball may not become pregnant the first time she's mated. If

*Owners who want racing dogs must be careful about choosing puppies. Some puppies will grow up to be racers, but most will be pet-quality dogs.*

that happens, take her back for a second mating the next time she's in heat.

Greyhound puppies are born nine weeks after the female is mated. During her pregnancy, your dog will need special care. Feed her a high-protein diet and give her plenty of gentle exercise. Beware of too much running, which can strain her heart. As the weeks go by, set up a *whelping* box in a quiet, warm place. This is where she will give birth. Give your dog a chance to get used to sleeping in the box.

Once the birth process begins, there's not much for you to do. Greyhounds are good mothers. Each puppy emerges headfirst, covered in its birth sac. The female will help the puppy break the sac. Then she'll bite through the *umbilical cord*. The blind, helpless puppy will weigh about a pound. As it wiggles around, the mother will lick the sticky fur to clean and warm the puppy. If the litter is a normal one, there will be eight to ten puppies.

Ask the vet to come by when the puppies are a few days old. They should be checked for defects. The vet can also remove their *dewclaws*. These are the useless claws that sometimes grow on the insides of a dog's legs. You'll also be reminded that the mother needs extra nutrition while she's nursing. Finally, the vet can tattoo an *ID number* inside each puppy's left ear. This number is used in racing. The tracks will use the ID number to identify the dog.

Greyhound puppies grow fast. At ten days, their eyes will open and they'll be able to hear noises. Instead of eating and sleeping all the time, they'll begin to move around on wobbly legs. At four weeks, the mother will *wean* her puppies. You can help by adding little balls of ground meat to the puppies' diet.

At eight weeks, you can send the puppies

off to new homes. If you see a future champion racer or show dog in the litter, you may want to keep it and train it yourself. You probably won't get rich, whatever happens—but you will have a good time.

# HOW DOES A GREYHOUND SIGNAL "I GIVE UP"?

Breeding and raising greyhounds was a whole new life for Mike. Ever since his parents decided to start a kennel, he had been reading about dogs. Reading was one thing, though, and working with 12 lively greyhounds was another. Mike saw lots of dog behavior he didn't understand.

"Mom," he said one day, "Chance is really weird. He's nine months old, and he's the biggest and strongest puppy we have. But every time he gets near old King, he acts like he's afraid. First, Chance crouches down and puts his tail between his legs. Then he reaches up

34

and licks at King's mouth. If King snarls at him, Chance rolls over on his back. Afterward, King just looks at Chance, sniffs once or twice, and walks away."

Barb Ryan smiled at her son. "You've just seen a behavior left over from the time when wild dogs lived in packs," she said.

"These are *domesticated dogs*, not a pack of wolves," Mike protested. "Chance should stand up for his rights."

"A dog's behavior is based mostly on instinct," Mrs. Ryan said. "Many of those instincts are left over from before dogs were domesticated. Now, if you think of our dogs as belonging to a pack, King is 'top dog.' Isn't that right?"

"Well, all the other dogs seem to stay out of his way," Mike agreed. "If he starts to howl, everyone else joins in."

Mrs. Ryan nodded. "Chance knows his place in the pack," she said. "Maybe he'll be able to beat King in a fight someday. But for now he doesn't dare risk it. If he lost, he'd become an outcast. So, Chance lets King know in dog language that he accepts his role as underdog."

"I guess that makes sense," Mike said. "Still, why does Chance have to act like a scared puppy? Couldn't he just wag his tail or something?"

As they talked, Mike went over to a whelping box that stood in a corner. He picked up a tiny, wiggly puppy, and Mrs. Ryan handed him a nursing bottle. Tanny was the "runt" in a large litter. The puppy's larger litter mates crowded him out when he tried to nurse. Mike had taken over the job of feeding him.

"If you think about it," Mrs. Ryan said, "Chance is acting just like Tanny. His instincts tell him King won't attack a small puppy. So he crouches down and licks at King's muzzle. Even if King wanted to attack him, the puppy 'act' would block the older dog's aggression."

Mike rubbed Tanny's fat stomach. The pup was doing well on his special diet of goat's milk and vitamins. "Will Tanny know how to stay out of trouble when he grows up?" he asked. "By living here with us, is he missing out on some of his lessons?"

Mrs. Ryan picked up a bag of dog food. "Tanny will be okay," she said. "What he doesn't know by instinct, he'll learn from the other dogs. Now, it's time to feed the rest of our pack."

Mike put Tanny back into his box. "Okay, let's go," he said. "I'll give Chance some extra vitamins to grow on. Once he takes over as top dog, we can train him for coursing."

*Only the best-trained and fastest dogs compete in greyhound races.*

# THE ANCIENT SPORT OF COURSING

On a cool Kansas morning, the crowd gathers around a grassy, fenced-off field. Two greyhounds named Star and Pyro wait in starting boxes at one end. Not far away, a

37

jackrabbit crouches in a wire box. People study the two dogs and lay a few bets. A day of greyhound coursing is about to start.

Two judges ride horses into the middle of the 150-by-450-yard field. Another judge leans out of a tower and gives the signal to begin. The jackrabbit pops out of its box and darts across the field. When it has a 30-yard head start, Star and Pyro are set free to take up the chase. The jackrabbit runs a zigzag course. It forces the dogs to make high-speed turns. Star slips and tumbles head over heels. He gets up quickly, but the other dog now has the lead. Pyro wins more points by turning the jackrabbit from its line of flight. Then, with a final desperate leap, the jackrabbit reaches the escape hatch. The dogs skid to a stop, panting from their run.

The judges signal that Pyro is the winner. The greyhound won points for speed, for turning the jackrabbit, and for coming close to catching it. Because the aim is to compete, not to kill, the dogs didn't lose points for letting the jackrabbit escape. Later in the day, Pyro will be matched against the winner of the next event. Sixteen dogs will race before the day is over.

Using fast dogs to chase game began thousands of years ago. Greyhounds, salukis, and whippets were bred for coursing. The sport came to Britain with the Romans, but by the 1500s it was more a slaughter than a sport. With four or more greyhounds pursuing it, the hare was almost always killed. During the reign of Queen Elizabeth I, new rules were written. Only two dogs were allowed to run at a time, and the hare was given a lead of 700 feet. Coursing became a passion with the British, who set up the first coursing society in 1776.

Opponents of coursing say it is a cruel "blood sport." They argue that the dogs always kill the hare if they catch it. Coursing's defenders answer by saying only one in four chases results in a kill. Those animals that are killed die at once of a broken neck. Still others point out that hunters shoot far more animals than are killed in coursing.

# THE GREYHOUNDS ARE RUNNING!

The crowd buzzes with excitement as handlers lead eight sleek greyhounds onto the

*Before a race, handlers lead their greyhounds to the starting boxes.*

track. Lights blaze down, turning night into day. Each dog is muzzled and wears a colorful numbered blanket. The handlers place the dogs in the starting boxes.

The mechanical rabbit comes to life, opening the starting gate. The eager greyhounds shoot out of their boxes. The rabbit zips around the curving track, staying just ahead of the leader. The dogs bump each other as they round the second curve. One dog is knocked off stride. It falls behind as the other dogs streak after the

40

*A greyhound race begins when the dogs eagerly shoot out of the starting boxes.*

*lure.* At the finish line, the winner edges out the second-place dog by a nose. From start to finish, the 500-yard race takes only 26 seconds.

People attend dog races for several reasons. Many come for the joy of watching the greyhounds run. They learn to recognize their favorite dogs, and it's exciting to see them win. Other fans come because it's legal to bet on the races. They study each race and buy a ticket on the dog they think will win. The dogs

41

*A lure swifty rounds a corner, closely followed by the racing greyhounds.*

are graded from *A* to *E*, so that all eight dogs in each race will be of roughly equal ability. Each time a dog wins a race, it moves up a grade. The track makes its money from entry tickets and from its share of the betting. The dog owners, of course, are competing for prize money.

What do the greyhounds get out of it? They just love to run.

# TRAINING A GREYHOUND FOR THE RACETRACK

Imagine for a moment you are raising a greyhound pup named Gulliver. A racing trainer tells you Gulliver has the look of a winner. You decide to train the dog to run at the local tracks. Who knows? Maybe Gulliver will win enough prize money to send you to college.

Because Gulliver is still a pup, your first task is to get him used to the lead. Clip a lead to his collar and take him out each day for a fast walk. If he pulls ahead, try to keep up. If he drags behind, pull him along. Gulliver will soon learn to stay beside you. Along with being good exercise, these one-mile walks train the puppy to ignore traffic noise and strangers. Put Gulliver's muzzle on each time you take him out. He may not like being muzzled, but he'll have to wear one when he races.

You'll be surprised to learn Gulliver must learn how to gallop. Fast walking is the first step, because it teaches him to move with his natural rolling body motion. At six months, Gulliver will be ready to gallop. Find a wide-open, grassy field and let him run with other dogs, if you can. He'll learn by watching them, and he'll get used to being bumped in a race. Running uphill develops Gulliver's hindquarters, but don't allow him to run downhill. Downhill runs build up the front shoulder muscles, but shorten his stride.

The training is becoming tougher now, so make sure Gulliver is perfectly fit. Increase the protein in his diet, and make sure he's neither overweight nor underweight. If all is well, try him on a training track. Show him the lure. Shake it to make it seem alive. Hold Gulliver until the lure moves away. Reward him when he gallops after the moving lure. Run these first trials during the day, but later on you'll have to train him after dark, too. Most racetracks operate at night, when the crowds are larger.

The next step is to teach Gulliver to run from a starting box with mechanical gates. Make it easy for him at first by leaving both gates open. Hold him yourself, and let him go when the lure takes off. After several trials, close the front gate. When Gulliver accepts that, close the back gate as well. Now's also a good time to introduce him to a circular track. Don't be surprised if he stops when the lure disappears around the curve. He'll soon learn to keep going, especially if you run him with more experienced dogs.

Once Gulliver has learned his lessons, he's ready to race. Now, only one question remains. Is he fast enough? There's a good way to find out. Enter him in a novice race and cheer him on to victory!

*After long hours of training, a greyhound is finally ready to compete in — and maybe win — its first race.*

# ▌ GLOSSARY/INDEX

side a greyhound's left ear so that it can always be identified.

**Incisors** 15—The nipping and cutting teeth that grow between the canines.

**Instinct** 24, 29, 35, 36—Natural behavior that is inborn in a dog.

**Litter** 23, 24, 31, 33, 34, 36—A family of puppies born at a single whelping.

**Lure** 40, 44, 45—Any device that tempts a greyhound to give chase. In dog racing, the lure is a mechanical rabbit.

**Molars** 15—The dog's back teeth, used for slicing and crushing.

**Muzzle** 14, 21, 36 — The nose and jaws of a dog. Also, a covering for an animal's mouth, used to prevent it from biting or eating.

**Olfactory Patch** 18—The nerve endings in the nose that provide a dog's keen sense of smell.

**Pedigree** 24—A chart that lists a dog's ancestors.

**Premolars** 15—The dog's back teeth, used for slicing and chewing.

**Puppy** 22, 23, 24, 25, 28, 29, 30, 31, 32, 33, 35, 36, 43—A dog under one year of age.

**Purebred** 24—A dog whose ancestors are all of the same breed.

#  GLOSSARY/INDEX